Finding an Apartment

by Stuart Schwartz and Craig Conley

Consultant:
Robert J. Miller, Ph.D.
Professor of Special Education
Mankato State University

CAPSTONE
HIGH/LOW BOOKS
an imprint of Capstone Press
Mankato, Minnesota

Capstone High/Low Books are published by Capstone Press
818 North Willow Street • Mankato, MN 56001
http://www.capstone-press.com

Library of Congress Cataloging-in-Publication Data
Schwartz, Stuart, 1945–
Finding an apartment/by Stuart Schwartz and Craig Conley.
   p. cm.—(Life skills)
   Includes bibliographical references and index.
   Summary: A guide to finding and choosing the right apartment, discussing such
topics as renting, leasing, and subleasing; roommates; pets; making a budget; the
responsibilities of the rental agreement; and how to read an apartment ad.
   ISBN 0-7368-0046-8
   1. Young adults—United States—Life skills guides—Juvenile literature.
2. Apartments—United States—Handbooks, manuals, etc.—Juvenile literature.
3. Rental housing—United States—Handbooks, manuals, etc. 4. Consumer education—
United States—Juvenile literature. [1. Apartments—Handbooks, manuals, etc. 2. Life
skills.] I. Conley, Craig, 1965– . II. Title. III. Series: Schwartz, Stuart, 1945– Life
skills.
HQ799.7.S37   1999
646.7'00835—dc21

                                                                              98-35114
                                                                                  CIP
                                                                                   AC

Editorial Credits
Christy Steele, editor; James Franklin, cover designer and illustrator; Michelle L.
   Norstad, photo researcher

Photo credits
Barb Stitzer Photography, cover, 4, 6, 8, 10, 14, 16, 18, 20, 22, 24, 26
Photophile/Mark E. Gibson, 12

Table of Contents

Chapter 1

Types of Apartments

People must make choices after they decide to live on their own. They must decide where to live and how much rent they can afford to pay. It is important that people understand all their choices before they rent an apartment.

People can rent private, semi-private, studio, or efficiency apartments. Private apartments are not connected to other apartments. Semi-private apartments are in buildings with other apartments.

Studio apartments have one large room and a private bathroom. The large room has a kitchen area, a bedroom area, and a living area. An efficiency apartment is a studio apartment that includes furniture.

Some people choose to rent furnished apartments. Others choose to rent unfurnished apartments. Both furnished and unfurnished apartments usually include major kitchen appliances such as a stove and a refrigerator. Some apartments also have a dishwasher.

Semi-private apartments are in buildings with other apartments.

Chapter 2

Rent, Lease, and Sublease

Some people rent apartments from month to month. They pay money to a landlord to live in an apartment. People who rent apartments by the month may move whenever they wish. But landlords may change the rent price from month to month.

Most people sign an agreement called a lease when they rent an apartment. Renters agree to live in an apartment for a certain length of time when they sign a lease. They also agree to pay the rent every month until the lease period is over. The landlord usually decides the length of time the lease covers. The landlord often cannot change the rent price until the lease is finished.

People sometimes sublease or sublet apartments. They take on the responsibilities of someone else's lease. People who move out before their lease periods are over might sublease their apartments. Then the people who sublease pay the rent.

People pay money to a landlord to live in an apartment.

Chapter 3

Roommates

People who cannot afford to live alone might decide to live with roommates. Roommates pay part of the expenses and share apartment space. Some people rent large apartments and have more than one roommate. They divide the expenses by the number of renters.

There are several ways to find roommates. Some people choose to live with friends or advertise for roommates in newspapers. Some people ask their friends if they know anyone who is looking for a roommate. Other people use roommate services. These services match people who have similar needs.

Roommates should get along with each other. It is important to choose roommates who have similar likes and dislikes. For example, people who keep their surroundings neat and clean should choose roommates who are neat and clean. Otherwise, roommates might have disagreements. People should think about such problems and talk about them before moving into an apartment together.

Roommates should get along with each other.

Chapter 4

What to Look For

People should decide which apartment features they need before searching for apartments. Important features include the number and size of rooms. A feature that is important to one person may not be important to another. For example, the size of a kitchen is important to people who like to cook.

Parking is another important feature. Some landlords do not offer parking. Some apartments have parking lots or parking garages. Many landlords charge renters for parking spaces or garages. Other landlords offer free parking.

People need to ask which features are included in the rent. Rent payments sometimes include utility costs such as heat and electricity. Other rent payments do not include utilities. Utility costs can be expensive. Some people cannot afford apartments that do not include utility costs.

Some apartments have parking lots or parking garages.

Chapter 5

Extra Features

Landlords sometimes offer apartments with extra features such as fireplaces or skylights. Other apartments have ceiling fans, carpets, or fancy light fixtures.

Extra features may be outside the apartments. Some apartments include small yards or patios. Apartments that do not have yards sometimes have porches. Landlords often give tenants storage spaces in basements or attics.

Some apartment buildings have extra features that all renters share. Buildings might have a laundry room with washers and dryers. Other extra features include swimming pools, tennis courts, and gyms. People can save money by using these features. For example, renters may use the gym in their apartment building. They might do this instead of paying membership fees to use other gyms.

Some apartments include small yards.

Chapter 6

Pets

Every landlord has rules about pets. Many do not allow pets in the apartments. Some landlords allow cats but not dogs while others allow only birds and fish. People with pets must ask landlords about pet policies before renting apartments.

Some landlords may allow renters to have pets if they pay a pet deposit. Renters give this money to landlords before moving into their apartments. Pets can stain carpets or scratch woodwork. Landlords use pet deposits to pay for any damage caused by pets. Landlords return deposits if renters' pets do not harm the apartments.

People should think about problems their pets may cause before they look for apartments. Neighbors often complain about noisy pets. People who own dogs that bark a lot should choose private apartments. People with dogs may want to rent apartments with open areas outside. Dogs can exercise in these places.

Landlords sometimes allow pets if renters pay a pet deposit.

Chapter 7

Making a Budget

People should make budgets when they decide to look for apartments to rent. Their budgets will show whether they can afford the apartments they want.

People should write down several possible rent amounts. They should also write down several security deposit amounts. People must pay deposits before they can move into the apartments. A security deposit is often the same amount as the rent payment. Landlords return the deposits if renters do not damage the apartments.

Utility costs are not usually included in the rent payment. The amounts people pay for utilities change each month. People should ask the landlord or other renters how much their utilities cost. They can write down these amounts in their budgets.

People should add all of the costs to see if they can afford the apartments they want. They should choose the best place for the least money.

People should make budgets when they decide to look for apartments to rent.

Chapter 9

Important Concerns

It is hard to find an apartment that has every feature a person wants. People should choose an apartment that meets most of their needs. An apartment's location is important. People should make sure their apartment is close to their work or school.

People should find out how well landlords take care of their apartment buildings. People should ask landlords who is responsible for making repairs in their apartment buildings. People should ask if anyone makes repairs on weekends.

Safety is also an important concern. People can check crime reports from local police departments. These reports can help people decide how safe an area is. Some apartment buildings have security guards to help keep people safe. All areas in apartment buildings should be well lighted. People should choose apartments in areas where they feel safe and comfortable with the neighbors.

People should ask landlords who makes repairs in their apartment buildings.

Chapter 10

Understanding Responsibilities

Renting an apartment is a big responsibility. Renters must make rent payments on time every month. They must keep the apartments clean and in good condition. Renters sometimes must pay for repairs or cleaning.

Leases or rental agreements list the responsibilities of the renters. Renters must follow the rental agreements. For example, some apartments do not allow pets. Renters cannot decide to buy pets after moving into these apartments.

Renters sometimes break the rules of their rental agreements. This is called breaking the lease. Landlords can force renters to move if they break their leases. Landlords can force renters to pay rent for the full period of their leases.

Renters also have the responsibility of being good neighbors. They should not play loud music or make noise that disturbs other renters.

Renters must keep their apartments clean and in good condition.

Chapter 11

Know Renters' Rights

Renters have certain rights. Discrimination is against the law. Discrimination is unfair treatment of others because of their age, race, gender, or other differences. For example, a landlord may discriminate by saying an available apartment has already been rented. Landlords also may discriminate by not renting to families with children.

Discrimination laws do not apply in all cases. They do not apply to landlords who live in buildings with fewer than five apartments. This is because such small buildings are like the landlords' homes.

Renters must find out about their rights. They should call their local fair housing office. Phone books have numbers for the U.S. Department of Housing and Urban Development (HUD). HUD makes sure landlords obey the laws. Lawyers or legal-aid offices can help people who have experienced discrimination.

Some landlords discriminate by not renting to families with children.

25

Chapter 12

Signing a Lease

People must sign a lease or a rental agreement after they find an apartment. They should read the lease carefully before they sign it. They should not sign the lease unless they understand and agree with everything it says.

The lease should include important information such as how long the person is agreeing to rent the apartment. It should state the rent amount and when the rent is due. The lease should explain what happens if a person breaks the lease and whether subleasing is allowed. The lease should list any features included in the rent payment such as utilities.

The lease should include the amount of any security or pet deposits renters must pay. It also should state when renters will get their deposits back.

Some rental agreements are spoken instead of written. But written leases or rental agreements give renters more protection. Then people cannot lie about the agreements.

People must sign a lease or a rental agreement after they find an apartment.

Terms Used in Apartment Ads

AC — air conditioner

appl — appliances (such as a stove or a refrigerator)

apt — apartment

avail — available (date apartment will be ready to rent)

BA — bathroom

BR — bedroom

elec — electricity

furn — furnished

incl — includes

kit — kitchen

LR — living room

sec dep — security deposit

unfurn — unfurnished

util — utilities

w/w — wall-to-wall carpeting

w/d — washer and dryer

Words to Know

deposit (di-POZ-it)—money a renter pays to a landlord before moving into an apartment; a deposit pays for any damage renters may do to apartments.

discrimination (diss-krim-i-NAY-shuhn)—unfair treatment of others based on age, race, gender, or other differences

efficiency apartment (uh-FISH-uhn-see uh-PART-muhnt)—a furnished, one-room apartment

lease (LEESS)—a written agreement between a landlord and a renter

private apartment (PRYE-vit uh-PART-muhnt) — an apartment that is not connected to other apartments

studio apartment (STOO-dee-oh uh-PART-muhnt) — an apartment with one large room and a private bathroom

sublease (SUHB-leess) — to take on the responsibilities of someone else's lease

To Learn More

Milios, Rita. *Independent Living*. The Life Skills Library. New York: Rosen Publications, 1992.

Sacks, Ed. *The Renters' Survival Kit*. Chicago: Dearborn Financial Publications, 1993.

Schwartz, Stuart, and Craig Conley. *Living on Your Own*. Life Skills. Mankato, Minn.: Capstone High/Low Books, 1998.

Useful Addresses

American Renters Association
P.O. Box 503490
Indianapolis, IN 46250-8490

Nationwide Landlord and Tenant Assistance Association
P.O. Box 41066
Phoenix, AZ 85067-0166

Internet Sites

HUD Home Page: Fair Housing—It's Your Right
http://www.hud.gov/fhe/fheact.html

The National Directory of Apartments and Rental Housing
http://www.rentsearch.com/

Nationwide Apartment Selector
http://www.aptselector.com/

Quick Links for Renting
http://www.insiders.com/relocation/quickren.htm

Renting an Apartment
http://www.metlife.com/Lifeadvice/Purchases/
  Docs/rentaptintro.html

Index